MAKING WATER

FUTUREPOEM BOOKS
NEW YORK CITY
2022

MAKING WATER

Laura Jaramillo

first edition | first printing
This edition first published in paperback by Futurepoem Books
P.O. Box 7687 JAF Station
NY, NY 10116
www.futurepoem.com

Executive Editor: Dan Machlin
Managing Editor: Carly Dashiell
Associate Editor: Ariel Yelen
Editorial Assistant: Aiden Farrell
Copyeditor: Marcella Durand
Guest Editors: Anne Boyer, Alissa Quart, Wendy S. Walters
Cover design: Everything Studio (www.everythingstudio.com)
Interior design: HR Hegnauer (www.hrhegnauer.com)
Typefaces: Optima

Printed in the United States of America on acid-free paper

This project is supported in part by the New York State Council on the Arts with the
support of Governor Kathy Hochul and the New York State Legislature. It is also
supported in part by public funds from the New York City Department of Cultural
Affairs in partnership with the City Council, as well as by The New York Community
Trust Harris Shapiro Fund, The Leaves of Grass Fund, and Futurepoem's Individual
Donors, Subscribers, and Readers. Futurepoem books is the publishing program of
Futurepoem, Inc., a New York state-based 501(c)3 non-profit organization dedicated
to creating a greater public awareness and appreciation of innovative literature.

Distributed to the trade by Small Press Distribution, Berkeley, California
www.spdbooks.org

In memory of Joseph Romano and Karyn Kay

What difference is there to a blind man between a man making water and one bleeding in silence?

—DENIS DIDEROT
in "Letter on the Blind for the Use of Those Who See," 1749

QUARRY

There's a will to drown consumer electronics

that's distinct from revolution. Local kids smoke spliffs and cliff jump

the quarry. To have perhaps re-encountered yourself in

anger, natural as infancy in water

*

It doesn't smell so somehow circulates quietly through generosity and

impermanence. Against the Law, which is Summer

There really is no discernible bottom. They described people they desired as *present* or, *so present*. Edged by jagged rocks and slime, the middle is sun traversing evening water. A pat description of beauty is that which cannot last. This empire's lumber is sadness.

Saplings and weed.

*

Afternoon's boredom/bodily anarchy. The Eno winds through land-locked towns to loop around the empire of mosquitoes

Hang a right at Citgo. To say she's present really means everyone else is just not really there. The thereminic cry of girls before they hit the water. Grind w/ their granite lichens to sand. Light scatters through the canopy as a disco ball throws light.

*

Lost for a time in the abstract forest of your name. Leave me now in the head-holler.

They ask us for herb we ask them questions. One keeps talking

so continually reveals himself as not from here maybe a leafier

suburb. Manic talk with droplets running down

your torso is the tell

*

Trailers now neater and quieter than the opening through trees

some spilt diamond substance blinks and chatters above

Skinny and taught, bronze and brown, ringlets heavy with lake

one narrates the spiritual properties of meth. Profane words

brush the thinkable. Communion quick becomes some other

rite with bodies rent

Water flips the sky's axis. The wild stars of diving and no sound. Two

of them were fucking in the lake and I thought it wasn't real because

you couldn't spangle your body in this mud with mine. To live utterly

in the airy realm of things and see with borrowed eyes

I've never liked anything more than time. The rites of spring

in the strip mall parking lot. What flesh can do in masses with

the violet day through the slats. A tendency to float de-realized

above the afternoon, bodies on the gravel

*

People ask if in America we eat only hamburgers. Dust that traverses

the sun's rays down to its depth

Worn rope swing hung from ever-younger quaking aspens.

She swings off in defiance the boys applaud a latent desire to

be the lone woman among men dimly recognized in the heavy

heat undivided the one of us who "won," not split

*

Everything I know is fragments swimming off into the

private world of women

AUTOIMMUNITY

Did you take the narcissistic parent's hand? The form should
contain everything to contain totality. I said yeah, you trade the hell
of winter there for the hell of summer here. The mind cannot
picture a chiliagon's one thousand sides. Last night we met the nicest
guy high on crack at Kroger. Frost killed the organics.

*

Failure not visible on body's surface yet. She picked up a small
magazine called *Time Cuts Us into Pieces*.

Autoimmunity. What difference is there to a blind man between one making water and one bleeding in silence? I urinated nineteen times Tuesday. A woman encounters a cockroach and knows being. Consumed thirteen hundred calories. Beauty is no small part.

Simulated care sunk in the circulatory system. To listen like babies
pink and swaddled, alone and far away. The velvet lather of voices
automated against your aura. Performed for other strangers who can't
sleep. So many years I wanted anyone at all
to touch my face

*

A language in which still life means *dead nature*

Time-lapse video traces peaches in a bowl from decay to

dust. To too often catch the weft of life

woven through bleeding since I was twenty-

five and friends began to die

*

Friendship's liquidity

The first prohibition is touch. The savage din made by her knees moving under spandex in the yard. Under her uniform skirt hitched up beneath the senses. After a soccer ball. The birds sing at night unbearable and real

Hematology. When you'd thought bone was the fundament a

year of infections. Announcing the presence of water steam rises off

pavement. In the throat a hitch locates the circulatory sigh of prone

bodies breathing in time. Together.

*

I write "devastation" in lieu of vomiting in your mouth. Having been

at all times the recipient and the perpetrator.

Time is water traversing bones. A moment of internal silence impossible the heart is an audible presence then. Bile liquid viscera half-liquid plasma semi-liquid and I'm so fucking thirsty

Because the intellect is sometimes obscured by passion or disease

or sleep. A girl-brained body embroidered with hormones

and sweat will escape utility. Let this account of what

imagination is, and why it is, suffice

BAD MAGIC

Her heart broke at the ugliness of the city as she approached it over the bridge. He left two years later. We left three years before. I will never return and have never left. Dreams are parallelisms alongside holding facilities and row homes I return

*

I sold most of my books. The city will forget my face tomorrow

The sins of a dreamer are never more than this:

you felt nostalgia for the unknown university

you just wanted to make your living in an ugly town

you willed to walk the streets

head crowned with fugitive thought

No longer quite young, you appear to yourself as a photograph
and the bad magic of Images fails you. Having never known your
beauty as a breathing being, a desolation appears to engulf you
the city's mirage walking hungry on wind cutting streets

*

I will never be so alone again as I was then
and it aches

All of history the story of its retraction. The squats and encamp-

ments taken over by the knifey glamour of filial names and economics,

the ecstasy of class and mirrored display. If the storage unit throws our

clothes and our letters in the trash, let us not live

in remembrance of them

*

Give it up for space

transmuted into time

By year three

Memory will become

Imagination tall as

loblolly pines

Yellow Schwinn Collegiate stolen. It's coming / it's going

in waves. So happy that day drinking Carlo Rossi at the Latvian

Cultural Center with poets I no longer know who I was in love with

or who loved me then besides my mother tho at 23

that had been the metronome

*

time is a melancholy sign system

money is a melancholy sign system

BREAD/WINE

Karyn, art is a beautiful fool who won't feed us. All the
theorists and writers in a swimming pool up by Columbia
sloshing in erotic intrigue. So memory must become the
bread. Here I am merely telling what you told me in life

*

Motherhood must be so saturated with the future solitude
of children

With memory the need for naïve solutions wanes. Your

laughter sets like a stain

*

The avant-garde buries its women like this

without flowers

Teachers are mothers for shattered cities. Or broken people
who say vulgar things to teens. I'll never go around that town again
trying to take up the fragments, trying to know its contusions and
lacerations

*

Looking out over the undulating sea of bored faces, he said, "I wanna
be a horse," equally bored

Pharmacy City's hands are sparkling clean and

Art in its pilled slumber

*

Gardens fertilized w/ women's forgotten body-ideas

Her dissertation books forever lining the window sill of a place

on midtown's west side. The long silent summer of my memory

watching kids dribble on the courts. When a teacher is laid waste,

a student is someone who can do nothing to help her

*

To drown, even to sink in the gorgeous difficulty of thought

BRAIN FLOWERS

Play classical music for the plants. Shale that once clasped
a shell to its heart ranged around the terrace. The gardener
cuts the bark to show me it bleeds a milk. Perfect stairs drawn
up into a rock, record of centuries

*

Rain/chicken pox/parasites/
the purity of boredom

Droplets drip down the tips, inverted translucent bells of
Forgetting. He's gone now, but had been to study *datura*
with the native people. She said "that dense atmosphere,"
there eyes stud the foliage

*

Vertigo
running down the spiral
stairs during light
rationing

Processed to powder in urban bars in the capital. Take
off your shoes give me your car keys sit on the ground.
The houses' high-walled enclosures blink with broken
bottle shards, bougainvillea below

*

Blue/green

/brown/

Transparent

the complete

anamnesis

an amnesia

Suppression of proper motor functions / the will
Memory loss serums introduced to the Garden by its
own fruit. They'll say look at the fallen world and
we'll look North

*

Flying ointments for young initiates. My eyes are open
but I can't *see*

Pielroja smoke climbs around afternoon sunlight. Sunday,
listen to him speak on the effect of rock v. classical in plant
growth. The "farm" a cement house in the jungle ground
gives way with orange ferment/fallen vine

Plant sentience explained in the book with a Rousseau

painting on its face. The lion eats his repast, behind

vine and bird of paradise. When asked to draw Eden,

she reproduced this

*

Days speaking one tongue, years another. It makes you

feel imaginary

Henri never saw the jungle. It was possible for him to

paint that place of total non-identity in which the lion sits.

I'm a primitive placeholder for meaning folded into the leaves

of experience

*

Imagination was that fallen middle

-class world

The heart muscle by nature weaker in the very tall circulating
blood through long limbs. Mocking the height of mountains
in North America, pointing to our Alps in Chile. It was early
when he died on the sofa

THRENODY FOR ISABEL

She's opening her eyes for you milk blue around brown iris

edge. Flowers on the road would perplex her violently,

a jolt back into "reality." That she would exit life through

the memory door, rather than the fleshy one

*

We enter into a world where color is all. The rest

already lost their language.

Lone conversationalist in the house, a man of unfailing

charm. Thin calories for the almost living oatmeal &

sugarcane. Nurse chatter, low televisual glow. Brain dissolved

over twenty-some years into body's entropy

*

Exquisite frequency at which toenails can be felt to push through

the meat.

To death you'll carry with you the reduced territory of a

consciousness once sovereign, but devastated. Tho no one

can define consciousness you'll remain on the

burnt plane holding a nagging ink

of an inkling

*

To mistake the cerebellum's ridges for the maze itself

Blood's about-ness suppressed by bad circulation. Each

hematoma's character determined by the presence

of yellow and green in its topography. A lake of blood

or a flooded golf course on her thigh

*

Symphony of lungs clasping air lends the oxygen a smoky

topaz density

Nerves run aground from flesh halo to scapular picture
of the saints aquiver printed hearts polyester batting felt
against bone. Lone woman in the family left for decades to do
the work of kindness, considered to be petting a corpse or at least
collection of half-beating organs

*

She's hiding in consciousness' audience. Chiefly, she's very
tired and wandered off

GATE AGENT

The airport is an envelope / notes to future selves write themselves.
I won't know you then, a problem of time lived through the
stomach, flora unbloomed in acid excess. Spit into my palm. Your genes
wash off but sensation makes grooves in my skin

*

I declare myself the most docile of animals carrying a still
life's worth of dead nature

Who had no essence? Who was liquid escaping through dis-
jointed plastic seams? Whose sequin hormones distend the
belly, catching light? Who was a spy crawling through a breach
in the language?

*

Enough bottle caps together
form a syntax

Double escalators in cold light read the hieroglyphs as aerogare

Weight of sleeplessness mapped onto disconnected corridors.

A girl bleeds from the mouth at border control. But also a budding

stillness, move quietly thru q's

Mi cuerpo alegre camina

Porque de ti lleva la ilusión

Como el agua

Como el agua

Como el agua

—Camarón de la Isla

MOLLYTALK

A dance for Adolfina. Television and daydreaming. *Girl, you'll be a woman soon. Please, come take my hand.* Her name so masculine and sentimental. An inauthentic flamenco is Mia Wallace's ecstasy. May our ugliness splay so violently into joy.

*

I became for a time a writer of reactionary lyric against free love. Then pissing with love I wept

What do you find in the eternal night of others' bodies that I
find in your heat. A drug that makes every skin gin-
clear diffracting like crystal is not anything but the monster
moon above Madrid

*

Flesh rearranged across the spine into fireworks of chemical
knowing at the neck's pivot

No one kept or encased in the velvet slipcase of my

desire, with an automated hinge. If I whispered I love you absent-

mindedly across the room I made myself a dumb machine,

body beset with the urge to die slowly like all other machines

The nun's bath in the cloister a five-foot-deep cement pit filled with water pumped in from the well. Still air and acacia shimmer in the silent patio. No figure more frightening than unbroken thought. Together in bathing costumes.

Light traverses the spaces where love like a sword has pierced

their bodies. An ocean of paper lanterns bobs on electronic

gales. The party of a piece with work, fucking of a piece with work.

We become knotted precisely where we try to undo

*

I, the worst of all, often can't fuck

don't want to work with my body

The sun comes up in an apartment and I've been vomiting through my nose. Sun pricking moorish fortress blinds and the marimba sample's edge sweetens that light. Subjecting my body, waiting for recognition

FEAST

Formica-covered furniture petroleum smolder into the night
sky dragging Ikea bookcases and side tables onto the metro to
feed the bonfires. A tall African clad in white leaps over a
Babel of burning rubble

*

Feed the sun fire, feed the sun language on the eve
of its weakening

Fire a particular way to dismember a thing. Compressed fibers
in particleboard, notebook with laminate cover, receipts. Guts—
what was tender pulp consumed the quickest. What was tender—
your name x 10

*

My wrist aches when I write now. Notebook a record
of tiny lacerations

To feel the permutations of night that garden behind the
monastery. Heady youth bloom perfume of worklessness and
revolutionary romanticism. The city for a year expressed itself
as a utopia of women and the work-free

*

A scrap of paper loses its structure in flame garlanded
around the names Lampedusa/Gibraltar

My imagination will walk in the City of Women

for life, weaving garlands

*

Continuous impossibility mottled by encounter. A blue

Mediterranean promise

*

A generosity that opens out onto another form of being.

She stopped loving me

exile

*

passenger /

Bad translator

Spy

LACRIMOSA

East Coast rentals carry those Florida plates bearing orange
blossoms, vermilion and white abundant promise in the
land of eternal night. Old immigrants buoyed on prosperity of
car dealerships prosperity of delis prosperity of dry cleaners

*

Cities of the east mortgaged to meanness and ice a whole life
and its ways expires w/out witness

To "make it" to Nassau from East New York blackout in '77
during the riots they were stealing tables / making worlds and he
defining what Puerto Rican-Sicilian brown skin wasn't in the
dark. Said, How we [the whites] train our dogs.

*

Slowly, Spanish is extinguished from their feelings

Ice cream pints stowed in Chevy's trunk, wrapped in blankets

selling to bodegas in the boroughs, driven against potholes and

chemical gales blown off Newtown Creek. Managing a

strip club at the edge of Corona

Little plaster angel hung on the door casts his eyes down at us the way

shag carpet devours light and sound. Bore the surname Romano, sun-

baked commoner in the empire's southern leg. Bore this ordinariness

not as the soul of dispossession but as the root of the normal

*

Abandoned rap CD bakes out in cash-bleached
suburban sunshine *white is right* to brittle coarsening

The double face of Gemini spits in the eye of sadness then folds in on itself, never to be known. But we admired Hendrix's moves like a flaming oil slick on the sea his light sliding and sparking against electric frame

Anointed king of the clan by the sweat of his brow. Sit out

on a folding chair getting umber in the sun. The same classic rock

that was never classic with the subwoofers on. Why

won't you come to him with your problems

*

By now, the whole coast's tangle of glittering traffic

mortgaged time to nothingness

When you became an invalid, you saw for the first time the world

reflected in the dog's lachrymose eye. We look out the Amtrak window

over the dun-colored lake to see it perfectly mirror the dun-colored sky

Carolina mold nestled quietly in the folds of our garments

*

And a swarming kinetic force goes out of this world

Because my feelings are a harp of ether

I came home to rest the day he resigned

*

Flesh

is against us he replaced the shape of his form

in the universe w/ the word Christmas. I kept thinking time

is reversible. She sd they lay down new carpet only

in the spot where it happened. Telluric cycles of feast say time

is renewed   flesh

is renewed he

is risen again but this isn't

it the skull's architecture blown over blankets

in precise fragments. No love for the broken body

in the Cult of Man which would fit together as a jigsaw

is some time-killing object what did that mean when

is the time to die

*

In the arms of my imagination

    a pietà where I talk to him feet wrapped in clean gauze

carefully wound by the hands of women. We washed each

inheriting accidentally another world

in that process where men's hearts

    wither leprously. If we lacked them we were born

      already our own fathers

If the matter of the broken body persisted

in the oyster-colored light

it was because he had risen and   was laughing, wearing sunglasses

    insisting like a bandaged

      zombie Lazarus it was a joke

Do the women dress you now in purple raiments

and greet you at the threshold in the morning

      washing your feet

*

They tell you to go down

into that deep witnessing and the whole edifice

/incoherence of self

splays out and resists   I'll tell you

mourning is Nothing

and Boredom. By January I had

become the soul of New Year connecting

vomit and tinsel through negative space

just that / Nothing

clapperless lead bell affixed to the lung

Time reveals its true face in ambient footfall

of dogs howling

across the neighborhood

away from idea   towards song

No one wants to be nothing

and no one wants to be nowhere

and yet we are dislocations

incidentally cut

with experience

Gliding empty on and off exit ramps almost in the middle

of my life still a student w/ no more than a dollar

in my pocket I've refused so much for sunny

investments in Beauty, or Memory

HANDEDNESS

Rubber bullets rebounding off the backs of passengers at Atocha. Which Nation really loves work? He climbed a pole rigged with cameras in Bahrain wearing a balaclava. Tectonic seizure continuous cuts. A Committed Poetry. He swung that hammer. No, which nation *really* loves work?

*

Lost for a time in the abstract country of your name. Leave me now in the head-house.

Just call me the LOL assassin, or forget to. Austerity is a metal

spike to adorn our vague tongue with acid dislocating speech.

English, the language of knives and incorporations,

the language of instruments

*

Always to work. I am a hammer broken

against work

Work and fortune are two symmetrical dreams. Taught after

becoming teachers to "think" our obsolescence. Hey you,

clearheaded not head full of clouds watch the cumuli sweep

the future

/ not here

*

All of nature changing outside the window. A clear sense of office /

destruction

The university a gray dream retreating on an infinite plane.

Voices losing their meat discussing *the body* as an already dead

thing. The presumed living operate imaginary hammers and

everyone's phone continually drops into jeweled

sucking mud

*

Walking out into the street / An end

To imagine or practice a new way of sensing. I believe this—

how language folding the color carnelian into music invented

curiosity. How everything in its vibrancy is bound and bucks

meaning, the world's intelligence in excess

of the instruments

*

Sovereignty climbs up my throat and I expel it from my body
again all its forms the victim the bohemian the child the dog
owner the tutor the citizen the anarchist the poet a simple
quaking disgust ribbed by
       control the diaphragm spasms

So many times collapsing under its weight
       taking responsibility for my own self
when I have never   been one

Nor is thought one
       but the world's discordant chorus
           showing how meaning is garlanded and
           undulates / round being
                   if you want it

You make me laugh

       I drift to sleep

       You say phrases

       I mimic your gestures

       which become the fabric of me

Dusk draws fiery orbs on the wall and play is the memory

of freedom

WARMACHINE

So much purple asleep in the green of the sea. Luminous Carolina
sky crossed with cumulus cotton balls. Colors recoil when military
choppers blow back waters' first ten veils. Today no planes circulate
above Ferguson, Missouri. Edge of vomit
edge of every thing

*

They were wrapping light around their bodies and shitting
in the water

Spraying sunscreen into the atmosphere because my not-body

replaces my torso with air and the warmachines' contours are

becoming in the honeyed light. Heavens rent with metal

sand kaleidoscopic beneath us

*

Swimmers applaud beckoning the machines

into the water

The special violence from which we suffer goes all pink and

green, holographic in the evening sun. That all of existence could

be a Pleasure Palace, that all of Survival could be a boot to the

neck of the other

*

Our time an orchestra heard in the distance

sinking

We were so beautiful that day, all consumer metaphysics and pink
meat ribboned with phosphorescent fat. I took thirty-seven pictures
of myself in the back seat to make sure I still existed

*

Animals on the road petrify when light hits their eyes

Let your body go like water. The car revolving our airborne
forms, leaves and mud revolving the car. Floating in silence with
its terror and force through the sinews. She understood then that
incoherence as dying
splayed through that violent will
to live

Curiously, the drone is a whale with no face. There
are frequencies inside the chest that hum in absolute fear
and it moves as a mantis moves cutting air with its
not-animal countenance

*

Pterodactyls circle and cacti hiss, edge of vomit edge of
everything

Heat maps mark the movement of blood-bearing bodies
across desert sand

*

The operators open
their inter-
faces ribbed with fire tipped in

blood the men
pull over

to peak over
the side of

a ditch crew
cut and rosy

the men
disappointed
we're not hurt
wanting to have
been heroes

or at least become

the one

holding

the terror and

force the fire and

percussive blow-

back the shrapnel

and tie cuffs the paper

work of modernity

the men perform

ICE

operations at

the Spahn Ranch

at Arivaca

at Tabernas

they'll fake out

a frontier in the

desert of the real

If they have to

Abide by some basic

banality

to "serve"

then oil the contours

of their physiques

The one man

with such a Barbie

-like arc in

his tit/

pectoral

muscle the technological veil

pneumatic

virtually

weightless Kevlar

condemned to bear

the melancholy

of Robocop's sensuous

pink lip the pilots

rip open

A breach in being

becoming war

gods in a sky

from which the

regular gods

have retracted

to rend the veil

of women only

to conceal

their own faces

so they may

never

witness themselves

being seen

by their marks

Air force sky measured in bits of space-time, all of powder

blue's tonalities measured as hubris. Isabel was undercover in the

auditorium when her husband in pressed uniform spoke eloquently

on the existence of aliens those

who would deliver us from this

*

Multiply the future by one hundred, then divide by history

SCHIZOMIRROR

for M.M.

A picture finishes by
abolishing its object
I watch her to see myself
holding a mirror
to the wave / infinity

*

Idolatry of the One will
shatter us into a million
pieces. Having stated *this
is nature* they wage glass
warfare

Mirror ringed with knives

Mirror ringed with fire

Mirror ringed with blood

So the abstract god can sub-

divide us into discrete forms

*

Amongst generalized psychic

disintegration / dim purpose

My people are the fisher-

women of stars swimming

the underground of history

Beauty is no small part they'll
say she's making herself into an
image ranged across glittering
paillettes showy and for
everyone but herself

*

When in fact, we are for
no one, but humanity in its
oceanic guise. And we worship
no Abstract White God. We
will cover the mirrors w/ thick
felt blankets carry them out to sea
w/ utmost care

SOME RAIN

The drug wanes and we're tiny animals with huge hearts in our
absurd chests racing against sleep against the circulatory
bang bang pressed together. Many Sundays pass into winter and no
knows what is a marriage

*

Our windows and doors will be so fat with moisture by May. I inhale a
mutual dust

The cat's mammal-need to be hailed from the next room

lest he keep yowling with lights off. Your name is an event

that happens in sound

not words

*

Waiting for recognition. Assure me I'm an image in your head-

holler

To breathe into this hole where I could write what it is to be

beside you. I will not write like him: to be wet with a decent

happiness

but approximate. Our hearts will transform

they will not stay

still, happiness is never decent

No one should know what is a marriage, what images hold us

in the light of other images, which are just ideas what is time

in which to languish and reappear, what is the perfect trouble

with which all images are veined which our bodies will live

in the light of for life which like water runs before all sense what

is grace against which we brush as images

$\qquad\qquad\qquad\qquad$ against other images,

in the black light of memory a velvet poster, a map of what

has been, remembered as what will be, which is false and fails to make

an image of the world so radiant and violent the world whose

light is breaking and scattered like our limbs across the beach the pieces

all the light which you collect for me at night

RIVER SOCIETY

In a skin-lined chassis listening for an Iron Goddess of Mercy's
transmissions. Light more sodden and amber every spring.
Eating gods' flesh and watching our bodies pass above us in a
darkened field above the loblolly pines

*

Everything lost persists. And love underwrites this

The oogles and Mexican families the older day trippers and
river witches gather in their camps on rock forms around the
banks. Archipelagos. Trash in the streambed and smoke on
the water fat black and white mosquitos skim the surface

*

To read nature as a rebus

Silky mold blossoms seep up the banks of rotting nitrate,

thru mute Memory Palaces thru torture gardens + phone records

thru dental x-rays + memoirs thru receipts + debits thru

every graven mark

*

Anomie. The quiet science of the eighteenth-century naturalists casting

miniatures of the Americas' flora in glass

*

You go to the river to escape society then you become a society

*

River bed aslither with baptismal snakes I sit peeing

in the shallows and centuries pass

    Gather your low magic

    Gather your animals

    Our bodies were never that lost Utopia

    just an oracle

And if we were images

it was only for a time   and they're ululating

    on water and broken by the wind

where again   they scatter

into perfect chemical geometries and the Zen hum

of this water   all the water that has ever been

    what's left to us in common

NOTES

"Quarry"

In the essay "Of Beauty," Francis Bacon wrote, "Beauty is as summer fruits, which are easy to corrupt, and cannot last." (2)

"Grind w/ their granite lichens to sand" deforms a line from Lorine Niedecker's poem "Wintergreen Ridge," where she writes "lichens / grind with their acid / granite to sand." (3)

"Autoimmunity"

A chiliagon is a geometric form with one thousand sides. Because we cannot picture each of the thousand sides in our minds all at once, Rene Descartes used the chiliagon as an example of a form that we understand through the intellect rather than imagination. (9)

Time Cuts Us into Pieces is the title of a zine by German artist Rosemarie Trockel, displayed as part of the exhibition "Rosemarie Trockel: A Cosmos," which ran at The New Museum in New York City in 2013. (9)

In Clarice Lispector's *The Passion According to GH,* a Brazilian woman sees a cockroach in the servant's quarters of her apartment and her profound disgust triggers an ecstatic meditation on existence. (10)

In Sam Taylor Wood's "Still life" (2001), we watch video footage of a classically composed still life of a bowl of peaches decomposing, growing fuzzy white mold until eventually disintegrating and then disappearing through sped up time-lapse video. (12)

The stanza on page 16 quotes from Aristotle's *De Anima*: "because imaginations remain in us and resemble the corresponding sensations, animals perform many actions under their influence; some, that is, the brutes, through not having intellect, and others, that is, men, because intellect is sometimes obscured by passion or disease or sleep. Let this account of the nature and cause of imagination suffice." (16)

"Brain Flowers"

Pielroja is the name of a Colombian cigarette brand founded in 1942 which has remained linked to national identity and to Colombian masculinity in particular. (31)

Peter Tompkins and Christopher Bird's *The Secret Life of Plants* (1973) made the controversial claim that plants grew toward the sounds of classical music, preferring them to the harsher sounds of popular genres like rock. (31-32)

"Mollytalk"

Maria Luisa Bemberg's *I, the Worst of All* (1990) is biographical film about the life of the seventeenth century Mexican poet and nun Sor Juana Ines de la Cruz, who was forced to renounce her worldly possessions after writing heretical interpretations of the Bible. Sor Juana's confessional letter to the Inquisitionis signed, "Yo, la peor de todas," or "I, the worst of all women." (48)

"Feast"

Federico Fellini's *City of Women* (1980) a middle-aged director confronts his cartoonishly sexist attitudes towards women and in doing so, confronts a feminist movement that no longer wishes to position him at the center of the world. (54)

"Lacrimosa"

The failure of New York City's power grid on July 13, 1977 resulted in a 25-hour blackout, during which residents of poor Black and Latino neighborhoods looted city stores. Early hip-hop DJs cite the looting as having supplied the technological basis—in the form of turntables, mixers, and microphones—for the eventual creation of hip-hop. (56)

"Warmachine"

The Tabernas desert in southern Spain was commonly used as a shooting location for Spaghetti Western films because of how much it resembled the deserts of the American West. Arivaca is a small town in Arizona on the border with Mexico that has become a hotspot for anti-immigrant militias. The Spahn Movie Ranch was an abandoned movie ranch that served as home to the Manson family in the late 1960s. (81)

"Some Rain"

"Be wet. / with a decent happiness" are lines from Robert Creeley's poem "Some Rain" (91)

"River Society"

"torture gardens" is from Jack Spicer's poem "Billy the Kid" (95)

ACKNOWLEDGMENTS

Pieces from this work have appeared in *The Brooklyn Rail, The Recluse, the tiny, So and So Magazine, Elderly Mag, Bone Bouquet, Talisman, Senna Hoy, Casa de las Américas,* and *Happy Monks* pamphlet series. A section of this work also appeared as a chapbook, *29 Waters,* published by Make Now Press, Los Angeles. Thank you to the editors who gave these poems their first homes.

Thank you to following the people who encouraged this book's extension into the world:

Marta Núñez Pouzols, Carla Hung, Michelle Helene Mackenzie, Jessica Q. Stark, Zach Levine, Navid Naderi, María Salgado, Paige Taggart, Lauren Hunter, Ryan Eckes, Alessandro Porco, Corinne Blalock, Kathryn L. Pringle, Wendy Trevino, Zaina Alsous, José Romero, Philip Stillman, Ara Shirinyan, Ted Rees, and Cynthia Arrieu-King.

And very special thanks to Ryan Vu who illuminates all things.